To parents and teachers

We hope you and the children will enjoy reading this story in either English or Spanish. The story is simple, but not *simplified,* so that both versions are quite natural. However, there is plenty of repetition for practicing pronunciation, for helping develop memory skills, and for reinforcing comprehension.

At the back of the book is a small picture dictionary with the key words and how to pronounce them. There is also a simple pronunciation guide to the whole story on the last page.

Here are a few suggestions on using the book:

- Read the story aloud in English first, to get to know it. Treat it like any other picture book: look at the pictures, talk about the story and the characters, and so on.

- Then look at the picture dictionary and say the Spanish names for the key words. Ask the children to repeat them. Concentrate on speaking the words out loud, rather than reading them.

- Go back and read the story again, this time in English *and* Spanish. Don't worry if your pronunciation isn't quite correct. Just have fun trying it out. Check the guide at the back of the book, if necessary, but you'll soon pick up how to say the Spanish words.

- When you think you and the children are ready, you can try reading the story in Spanish only. Ask the children to say it with you. Ask them to read it only if they are eager to try. The spelling could be confusing and put them off.

- Above all, encourage the children to try it, and give lots of praise. Little children are usually quite unself-conscious and this is excellent for building up confidence in a foreign language.

First edition for the United States, its dependencies, Canada, and the Philippines published in 2006 by Barron's Educational Series, Inc. Text and illustrations © Copyright 2005 by *b small publishing*

Address all inquiries to:
Barron's Educational Series, Inc. • 250 Wireless Boulevard • Hauppauge, New York 11788 • **http://www.barronseduc.com**

ISBN-13: 978-0-7641-5875-9   ISBN-10: 0-7641-5875-9
Library of Congress Catalog Card Number 2005921558

Printed in China
9 8 7 6 5 4 3 2 1

Space postman

El cartero espacial

Lone Morton

Pictures by Martin Ursell
Spanish by Rosa María Martín

BARRON'S

Captain Crater climbs
into his spaceship.
He is the space postman.

El capitán Cráter sube
a su nave espacial.
Él es el cartero espacial.

He turns the blue dial to the left
Tuerce el mando azul a la izquierda

and the yellow dial to the right.
y el mando amarillo a la derecha.

He presses the green button:
Aprieta el botón verde:

GO!
¡EN MARCHA!

BLAST OFF!

¡DESPEGUE!

Whoosh! He takes off into the sky.

¡Bruuum! Sube al cielo.

His first stop is Planet Fizz.
He has a letter for Princess Shush.

Su primera parada es el planeta Fizz.
Tiene una carta para la princesa Shush.

It's an invitation to a wedding.
She is very happy.

Es una invitación para una boda.
Está muy contenta.

Second stop: Planet Ooloo.
He has a package for Farmer Flop.

Segunda parada: el planeta Ooloo.
Tiene un paquete para el granjero Flop.

It's a big book.
He is very happy.

Es un libro grande.
Está muy contento.

The next stop is Planet Astro.
He has a postcard for Blop.

La próxima parada es el planeta Astro.
Tiene una postal para Blop.

Oh, no!
¡Oh, no!

On the way, the door opens…
En el camino, la puerta se abre…

…and the mailbag falls out!
¡…y la bolsa del correo se cae!

Captain Crater lands on Planet Astro.
But there is no mailbag.

El capitán Cráter aterriza
en el planeta Astro.
Pero la bolsa del correo no está.

"I am going to look for it," he says
to Blop. "But I will come back."

"Voy a buscarla", le dice
a Blop. "Pero volveré".

He flies east.
Vuela al este.

He flies west.
Vuela al oeste.

He flies north and then south.
Vuela al norte y después al sur.

But he can't find the mailbag anywhere.

Pero no puede encontrar la bolsa del correo por ninguna parte.

"Bleep, bleep, bleep," his phone rings.

"Ring, ring, ring", suena su teléfono.

"Hello, hello. It's the space police.
We have found a mailbag...

"Hola, hola. Es la policía espacial.
Hemos encontrado una bolsa del correo...

...hanging from a star!"

¡...colgada en una estrella!"

Captain Crater is very happy.

El capitán Cráter está muy contento.

Blop's postcard is from
his twin brother, Blip.

La postal de Blop es de
su hermano gemelo Blip.

"He's arriving tomorrow on the
Space Bus!"
Blop is very happy.

"¡Llega mañana en el autobús
espacial!" dice Blop. Está contento.

Pronouncing Spanish

Don't worry if your pronunciation isn't quite correct.
The important thing is to be willing to try.

The pronunciation guide is based on the Spanish accent used
in Latin America. Although it cannot be completely accurate,
it certainly will be a great help.

• Read the guide as naturally as possible, as if it were English.

• Put stress on the letters in *italics*, as in pah-*keh*-teh.

If you can, ask a Spanish-speaking person to help and move on as
soon as possible to speaking the words without the guide.

Note: Spanish adjectives usually have two forms, one for masculine
and one for feminine nouns, as in **contento** and **contenta**.

Words Las palabras
lahs pah-*lah*-brahs

star
la estrella
lah ehs-*treh*-yah

sky
el cielo
ehl see-*eh*-loh

space bus
el autobús espacial
ehl ow-toh-*boos* ehs-pah-see-*ahl*

spaceship
la nave espacial
lah *nah*-veh ehs-pah-see-*ahl*

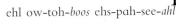

postman

el cartero
ehl kahr-*teh*-roh

mailbag

la bolsa del correo
lah *bohl*-sah dehl kohr-*reh*-oh

postcard

la postal
lah pohs-*tahl*

big

grande
grahn-deh

happy

contento/ contenta
kohn-*tehn*-toh/kohn-*tehn*-tah

parcel

el paquete
ehl pah-*keh*-teh

letter

la carta
lah *kahr*-tah

book

el libro
ehl *leeb*-roh

north
el norte
ehl *nohr*-teh

west
el oeste
ehl ow-*ehs*-teh

east
el este
ehl *ehs*-teh

south
el sur
ehl soor

left
izquierda
ees-kee-*ehr*-dah

right
derecha
deh-*reh*-chah

blue
azul
ah-*sool*

yellow
amarillo/
amarilla
ah-mah-*ree*-yoh/
ah-mah-*ree*-yah

green
verde
vehr-deh

A simple guide to pronouncing this Spanish story

El cartero espacial
ehl kahr-*teh*-roh ehs-pah-see-*ahl*

El capitán Cráter sube a su nave espacial.
ehl kah-pee-*tahn* krah-tehr *soo*-beh ah soo *nah*-veh ehs-pah-see-*ahl*

Él es el cartero espacial.
ehl ehs ehl kahr-*teh*-roh ehs-pah-see-*ahl*

Tuerce el mando azul a la izquierda
too-*ehr*-seh ehl *mahn*-doh ah-*sool* ah lah ees-kee-*ehr*-dah

y el mando amarillo a la derecha.
ee ehl *mahn*-doh ah-mah-*ree*-yoh ah lah deh-*reh*-chah

Aprieta el botón verde:
ah-pree-*eh*-tah ehl boh-*tohn* vehr-deh

¡EN MARCHA!
ehn *mahr*-chah

¡DESPEGUE!
dehs-*peh*-geh

¡Bruuum! Sube al cielo.
broom, *soo*-beh ahl see-*eh*-loh

Su primera parada es el planeta Fizz.
soo pree-*meh*-rah pah-*rah*-dah ehs ehl plah-*neh*-tah feez

Tiene una carta para la princesa Shush.
tee-*eh*-neh *oo*-nah *kahr*-tah *pah*-rah lah preen-*seh*-sah shoosh

Es una invitación para una boda.
ehs *oo*-nah een-vee-tah-see-*ohn* *pah*-rah *oo*-nah *boh*-dah

Está muy contenta.
ehs-*tah* mwee kohn-*tehn*-tah

Segunda parada: el planeta Ooloo.
seh-*goon*-dah pah-*rah*-dah: ehl plah-*neh*-tah *oh*-loh

Tiene un paquete para el granjero Flop.
tee-*eh*-neh oon pah-*keh*-teh *pah*-rah ehl grahn-*heh*-roh flop

Es un libro grande.
ehs oon *lee*-broh *grahn*-deh

Está muy contento.
ehs-*tah* mwee kohn-*tehn*-toh

La próxima parada es el planeta Astro.
lah *proh*-xee-mah pah-*rah*-dah ehs ehl plah-*neh*-tah *ahs*-troh

Tiene una postal para Blop.
tee-*eh*-neh *oo*-nah pohs-*tahl* *pah*-rah blop

¡Oh, no!
oh, noh

En el camino, la puerta se abre…
ehn ehl kah-*mee*-noh, lah *pwehr*-tah seh ah-breh

¡…y la bolsa del correo se cae!
ee lah *bohl*-sah dehl kohr-*reh*-oh seh *kah*-eh

El capitán Cráter aterriza en el planeta Astro.
ehl kah-pee-*tahn* *krah*-tehr ah-tehr-*ree*-sah ehn ehl plah-*neh*-tah *ahs*-troh

Pero la bolsa del correo no está.
peh-roh lah *bohl*-sah dehl kohr-*reh*-oh noh ehs-*tah*

"Voy a buscarla", le dice a Blop, "Pero volveré".
voh-ee ah boos-*kahr*-lah, leh *dee*-seh ah blop, *peh*-roh vohl-veh-*reh*

Vuela al este. Vuela al oeste.
voo-*eh*-lah ahl *ehs*-teh, voo-*eh*-lah ahl oh-*ehs*-teh

Vuela al norte y después al sur.
voo-*eh*-lah ahl *nohr*-teh, voo-*eh*-lah ahl soor

Pero no puede encontrar la bolsa del correo por ninguna parte.
peh-roh noh *pweh*-deh ehn-kohn-*trahr* lah *bohl*-sah dehl kohr-*reh*-oh pohr neen-*goo*-nah *pahr*-teh

"Ring, ring, ring", suena su teléfono.
reeng, reeng, reeng, *sweh*-nah soo teh-*leh*-foh-noh

"Hola, hola. Es la policía espacial.
oh-lah, *oh*-lah, ehs lah poh-lee-*see*-ah ehs-pah-see-*ahl*

Hemos encontrado una bolsa del correo…
eh-mohs ehn-kohn-*trah*-doh *oo*-nah *bohl*-sah dehl kohr-*reh*-oh

¡…colgada en una estrella!"
kohl-*gah*-dah ehn *oo*-nah ehs-*treh*-yah

El capitán Cráter está muy contento.
ehl kah-pee-*tahn* *krah*-tehr ehs-*tah* mwee kohn-*tehn*-toh

La postal de Blop es de su hermano gemelo Blip.
lah pohs-*tahl* deh blop ehs deh soo ehr-*mah*-noh *heh*-meh-loh blip

"¡Llega mañana en el autobús espacial!"
yeh-gah mahn-*yah*-nah ehn ehl ow-toh-*boos* ehs-pah-see-*ahl*

¡Blop está muy contento!
blop ehs-*tah* mwee kohn-*tehn*-toh